Punctuation is. boring and dull and rarely, discussed, very few people. understand the rules and even. fewer care: to understand without punctuation; however written communication becomes! unnecessarily—confusing a road without roadsigns "No" reader. should have to decipher? poorly, punctuated, prose, do you agree:

Stalking the Wild Semicolon

EASY GUIDE TO PUNCTUATION

William Myatt

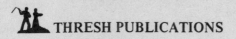 THRESH PUBLICATIONS

Printed in the United States of America

Thresh Publications
441-443 Sebastopol Avenue
Santa Rosa, CA 95401

Library of Congress Cataloging in Publication Data

Myatt, William, 1948—
  Stalking the wid semicolon.

  1. English language—Punctuation. I. Title.
PE1450.M9   421   76-15560
ISBN 0-913664-09-X

CONTENTS

INTRODUCTION

I wrote this in mild desperation. My students knew very little about punctuation and cared less. I needed some sort of organized presentation, but as fascinating subjects go, punctuation ranks slightly below appendicitis. Because everything that I had read about punctuation, no matter how helpful, was also terrifically dull, I consulted my own strange mind. This book is my brief, cheap, and slightly weird effort to grease up a dry subject.

The student response was excellent. Best of all, their skills improved and we were able to move on to immensely more interesting subjects.

STALKING THE WILD SEMICOLON

Punctuation is a drag to learn, a bigger drag to teach, and the biggest drag of all if you write anything without using it properly. Punctuation is necessary. When we speak, we pause and emphasize with our voices; when we write, we pause and emphasize with punctuation marks. What follows is a summary of the most commonly used and abused punctuation marks. It is not intended to be totally comprehensive, or even totally sane. It is intended to be used as a handy, if unorthodox, guide to punctuation. If you want to be a genuine punctuation freak, harrass a teacher or librarian into suggesting a good source book on style (I like *A Manual for Writers* by Kate Turabian — no respectable bookstore is without a copy), go to a mountain retreat or quiet corner, and freak out on how fascinating punctuation can really be.

Many rules of punctuation are, like the language, neither absolute nor clearly definable. After you have capitalized the first word of every new sentence however, there are a few absolutes and one is about our old friend the

. **PERIOD**

Used to end all sentences? No! *Used to end all declarative sentences or abbreviations* (Mr., Ms., etc.). If you do not understand periods, consult either a good English teacher or a good gynecologist. Whatever you do, do not get the two confused. English teachers blush easily.

?   QUESTION MARK

Used to end all sentences!
No. *Used to end all sentences which ask a direct
question.* Got it?

! EXCLAMATION POINT

Used to end all sentences. No? *Used to add special emphasis or excitement to phrases or sentences.* But! Be careful with exclamation points! Unless used very sparingly, exclamation points can diminish the effects of good prose! There is nothing exciting about too many exclamation points! If you find that hard to believe, look at any comic book!

, COMMA

Used to indicate a natural division or slight pause in a sentence. Commas are real toughies. Commas are used to tell the reader when to pause within a sentence, such as in a list of three or more words in a series—blood, sweat, and tears; the butcher, the baker, and the candlestick-maker. (The most, common, error, of most beginning writers is, to use entirely, too many, commas.) If you are confused, simply write your paper and use no commas. Then read the completed paper aloud to yourself and let your ear tell you when a pause, and therefore where a comma, is needed. A popular song entitled "My Girl Bill" hit the top ten for several weeks, because of one sneaky comma which is not revealed until the end of the song ("She's my girl, Bill"). Now if some guy can sell thousands of records with one little comma, imagine what you could do with a semicolon.

; SEMICOLON

Used to indicate a major division in a sentence in which a more distinct separation is felt than would be indicated by a comma. With a semicolon everything to the right of the semicolon is roughly equal to everything to the left; everything to the left is roughly equal to everything to the right. Now you are getting confused. Sometimes, a comma will work; sometimes, a semicolon works better. Semicolons are handy gadgets for use when you feel that two or more parts of a sentence are too different to be tied together by a comma, and too alike to be separated by a period. But beware because semicolons are cute and fun to make. People have been known to become infatuated with semicolons. Overindulgence in semicolons can lead to dizziness, shortness of breath, hairy palms and government intervention. In the interest of legalizing semicolons, read books, magazines and aerosol cans; pay attention to how and when other writers use semicolons; eventually you will understand the difference between commas and semicolons. (If you are *still* confused, then simply do not use semicolons. People have been known to live their entire lives without ever using one.)

:   COLON

Used to mark a major break in a sentence and to indicate that what follows is an elaboration or summation of what precedes it. (Any humor about colons might be offensive.) A colon is slightly easier to figure out than commas and semicolons: everything that follows a colon is an elaboration of what preceded it. Everything to the right of the colon adds further color or description or clarity to the statement to the left of the colon.

In summary:
1) colons mark major breaks in sentences;
2) colons signal an elaboration of the statement preceding the colon;
3) colons introduce a formal summation (and are signalled by words or phrases such as: "such as," "as follows," "in summary," and so on).

- HYPHEN

Used to connect parts of some compound words or the parts of a word divided for any reason. Some words are always hyphenated, but I cannot hand-pick any one of them as an example. One small rule: two words which do not normally form a hyphenated word, when put together and used as an adjective are tied together with a hyphen. Huh? Well, a salesman with a salespitch which is short and sweet can be said to have a short-sweet salespitch. A politician who never answers a question but always beats around the bush instead can be called (among other things) a beat-around-the-bush politician. (My brother-in-law who was a two-time all-star in his neighborhood's drink-her-under-the-table contest finally met his match when he fell in love with a filly from Philly who gave him her come-hither-go-away-closer look.)

Hyphens are most often used when a word must be broken and continued on the next line. If you see that you will have to end a line in the middle of a word, consult your dictionary for the proper syllable breaks for that word. *Never* hyphenate one-syllable words.

– DASH

Used to note a break in a sentence or hesitation in an utterance. A dash is often interchangeable with a colon and sometimes interchangeable with a comma—but not always. A dash indicates an abrupt break—an interjection—in a sentence. It is also used for emphasis. For many writers it is an important tool—the most important punctuation tool—for emphasis. When typing, a dash is made by hitting the hyphen key twice (formula: one hyphen makes a word; two hyphens make a dash; four dashes make a relay race)

“ ” “ ” “ ” “ ” “ ” “ ” “ ” “ ” “ ” “ ” “ ” “ ” “
“ ” “ ” “ ” “ ” “ ” “ ” “ ” “ ” “ ” “ ” “ ” “ ” “
“ ” “ ” “ ” “ ” “ ” “ ” “ ” “ ” “ ” “ ” “ ” “ ” “
“ ” “ ” “ ” “ ” “ ” “ ” “ ” “ ” “ ” “ ” “ ” “ ” “
“ ” “ ” “ ” “ ” “ ” “ ” “ ” “ ” “ ” “ ” “ ” “ ” “
“ ” “ ” “ ” “ ” “ ” “ ” “ ” “ ” “ ” “ ” “ ” “ ” “
“ ” “ ” “ ” “ ” “ ” “ ” “ ” “ ” “ ” “ ” “ ” “ ” “
“ ” “ ” “ ” “ ” “ ” “ ” “ ” “ ” “ ” “ ” “ ” “ ” “
“ ” “ ” “ ” “ ” “ ” “ ” “ ” “ ” “ ” “ ” “ ” “ ” “
“ ” “ ” “ ” “ ” “ ” “ ” “ ” “ ” “ ” “ ” “ ” “ ” “
“ ” “ ” “ ” “ ” “ ” “ ” “ ” “ ” “ ” “ ” “ ” “ ” “
“ ” “ ” “ ” “ ” “ ” “ ” “ ” “ ” “ ” “ ” “ ” “ ” “
“ ” “ ” “ ” “ ” “ ” “ ” “ ” “ ” “ ” “ ” “ ” “ ” “
“ ” “ ” “ ” “ ” “ ” “ ” “ ” “ ” “ ” “ ” “ ” “ ” “
“ ” “ ” “ ” “ ” “ ” “ ” “ ” “ ” “ ” “ ” “ ” “ ” “
“ ” “ ” “ ” “ ” “ ” “ ” “ ” “ ” “ ” “ ” “ ” “ ” “
“ ” “ ” “ ” “ ” “ ” “ ” “ ” “ ” “ ” “ ” “ ” “ ” “
“ ” “ ” “ ” “ ” “ ” “ ” “ ” “ ” “ ” “ ” “ ” “ ” “
“ ” “ ” “ ” “ ” “ ” “ ” “ ” “ ” “ ” “ ” “ ” “ ” “
“ ” “ ” “ ” “ ” “ ” “ ” “ ” “ ” “ ” “ ” “ ” “ ” “
“ ” “ ” “ ” “ ” “ ” “ ” “ ” “ ” “ ” “ ” “ ” “ ” “
“ ” “ ” “ ” “ ” “ ” “ ” “ ” “ ” “ ” “ ” “ ” “ ” “
“ ” “ ” “ ” “ ” “ ” “ ” “ ” “ ” “ ” “ ” “ ” “ ” “
“ ” “ ” “ ” “ ” “ ” “ ” “ ” “ ” “ ” “ ” “ ” “ ” “
“ ” “ ” “ ” “ ” “ ” “ ” “ ” “ ” “ ” “ ” “ ” “ ” “
“ ” “ ” “ ” “ ” “ ” “ ” “ ” “ ” “ ” “ ” “ ” “ ” “
“ ” “ ” “ ” “ ” “ ” “ ” “ ” “ ” “ ” “ ” “ ” “ ” “
“ ” “ ” “ ” “ ” “ ” “ ” “ ” “ ” “ ” “ ” “ ” “ ” “
“ ” “ ” “ ” “ ” “ ” “ ” “ ” “ ” “ ” “ ” “ ” “ ” “
“ ” “ ” “ ” “ ” “ ” “ ” “ ” “ ” “ ” “ ” “ ” “ ” “
“ ” “ ” “ ” “ ” “ ” “ ” “ ” “ ” “ ” “ ” “ ” “ ” “
“ ” “ ” “ ” “ ” “ ” “ ” “ ” “ ” “ ” “ ” “ ” “ ” “
“ ” “ ” “ ” “ ” “ ” “ ” “ ” “ ” “ ” “ ” “ ” “ ” “
“ ” “ ” “ ” “ ” “ ” “ ” “ ” “ ” “ ” “ ” “ ” “ ” “
“ ” “ ” “ ” “ ” “ ” “ ” “ ” “ ” “ ” “ ” “ ” “ ” “
“ ” “ ” “ ” “ ” “ ” “ ” “ ” “ ” “ ” “ ” “ ” “ ” “
“ ” “ ” “ ” “ ” “ ” “ ” “ ” “ ” “ ” “ ” “ ” “ ” “
“ ” “ ” “ ” “ ” “ ” “ ” “ ” “ ” “ ” “ ” “ ” “ ” “
“ ” “ ” “ ” “ ” “ ” “ ” “ ” “ ” “ ” “ ” “ ” “ ” “
“ ” “ ” “ ” “ ” “ ” “ ” “ ” “ ” “ ” “ ” “ ” “ ” “
“ ” “ ” “ ” “ ” “ ” “ ” “ ” “ ” “ ” “ ” “ ” “ ” “
“ ” “ ” “ ” “ ” “ ” “ ” “ ” “ ” “ ” “ ” “ ” “ ” “

" QUOTATION MARK

Used to indicate the beginning and end of a quotation. What more can be said? Some more can be said. Occasionally, writers will put quotation marks around words to give those words or phrases special emphasis. Frequently, "amateur" writers will "dabble" with all kinds of "cutesy" words and phrases and "surround" everything but "the kitchen sink" with "those" quotation marks. As bad writing habits go, it's one of "the worst." Quotation marks are also used around some titles. Read on.

ics italics italics italics italics italics italics italics italics italics
ics italics italics italics italics italics italics italics italics italics
ics italics italics italics italics italics italics italics italics italics
ics italics italics italics italics italics italics italics italics italics
ics italics italics italics italics italics italics italics italics italics
ics italics italics italics italics italics italics italics italics italics
ics italics italics italics italics italics italics italics italics italics
ics italics italics italics italics italics italics italics italics italics
ics italics italics italics italics italics italics italics italics italics
ics italics italics italics italics italics italics italics italics italics
ics italics italics italics italics italics italics italics italics italics
ics italics italics italics italics italics italics italics italics italics
cs italics italics italics italics italics italics italics italics italics
cs italics italics italics italics italics italics italics italics italics
cs italics italics italics italics italics italics italics italics italics
cs italics italics italics italics italics italics italics italics italics
cs italics italics italics italics italics italics italics italics italics
cs italics italics italics italics italics italics italics italics italics
cs italics italics italics italics italics italics italics italics italics
cs italics italics italics italics italics italics italics italics italics
cs italics italics italics italics italics italics italics italics italics
cs italics italics italics italics italics italics italics italics italics
cs italics italics italics italics italics italics italics italics italics
cs italics italics italics italics italics italics italics italics italics
cs italics italics italics italics italics italics italics italics italics
cs italics italics italics italics italics italics italics italics italics
cs italics italics italics italics italics italics italics italics italics
cs italics italics italics italics italics italics italics italics italics
cs italics italics italics italics italics italics italics italics italics
cs italics italics italics italics italics italics italics italics italics
cs italics italics italics italics italics italics italics italics italics
cs italics italics italics italics italics italics italics italics italics
cs italics italics italics italics italics italics italics italics italics
cs italics italics italics italics italics italics italics italics italics
cs italics italics italics italics italics italics italics italics italics
cs italics italics italics italics italics italics italics italics italics

ITALICS

Used to emphasize important words or sentences and titles. All of the key one-sentence definitions in this book are italicized. (We mortals with pens and typewriters have to <u>underline</u> when we italicize. Typesetters have a special slanted type for italics.) Italics go with the titles of big things; quotation marks go with the little things. "The Bear" is a short story in Faulkner's book entitled *Go Down Moses*. "How to Beat Inflation" is an article in *Redbook* magazine. "Ariel" is a poem in Sylvia Plath's book of poems entitled *Ariel*. "The Pursuit of Happiness" is an episode of the *Civilisation* television series. "Changes" is a song on the album entitled *Mother Lode*. The *Queen Mary* is a big ship. The "Queen Bruce" is my cousin's crummy rowboat. Foreign words and phrases are also italicized, *bien entendu*. Foreign phrases are also a pain in the thesaurus. Avoid them. Leave them for the scholars, critics, English department chairmen and others who strive to impress each other and confuse the masses.

( ) PARENTHESES

Used to mark off inter-jected or explanatory remarks. Parentheses are not quite like dashes (or relay races). Parentheses indicate (usually) less abrupt interjections and allow the writer to include some remarks which might be considered extraneous or off the subject otherwise. (I have taken some classes in which the entire course should have been put in parentheses.)

' APOSTROPHE

Used to indicate the omission of one or more letters in a word; used to indicate the plural form of abbreviations and symbols; used to indicate the possessive form of most words. Apostrophes get misplaced a lot. They are easiest to remember with abbreviations, as in one M.D. plus one M.D. equals two M.D.'s, or there are 1000's of M.D.'s. Warning: *only* abbreviations, numbers and symbols are pluralized with 's. Apostrophes in all other situations mean something completely different.

For example, the apostrophe stands for omitted letters in contractions (you + are = you're; it + is = it's. Now that you know about contractions, use them sparingly).

The possessive (ownership) case is what gets sticky. Usually, if a word is singular or does not end with an *s*, add 's to form the possessive (if one girl has a jackhammer, it is the girl's jackhammer; if several women own a jackhammer, it is the women's jackhammer). If a word is plural and ends with an *s*, make it possessive by putting the apostrophe after the *s* (if two girls share a jackhammer, it is the girls' jackhammer). A debate arises over the names of people ending in *s*. Some people want to go the Jones' house for dinner, others to the Jones's house, and still others to the Joneses' house. I prefer the Jones' house. I suggest we all go the Smiths' house and settle this dispute with fountain pens at twenty paces.

PUNCTUATION IS NOT
A SERIES OF DUMB RULES

There is more of course, but this is enough for all the basic moves. If you are still hungry, look up ellipsis and asterisk at your local library. Or look in Turabian's *Manual* for a few shortcuts in punctuation, how to put a quotation within a quotation, or whatever else turns you on.

Punctuation marks are simply one more way that a writer can clarify and add variety to prose. You may have noticed some overlap in definitions and purposes of certain punctuation marks. That overlap is good, because it allows the writer to change subtly the effects of words and phrases. Indeed, the same sentence can be rewritten several times using a different scheme of punctuation (therefore creating a slightly different effect) each time. The warning with semicolons applies to all forms of punctuation, all forms of sentence patterns, and all forms of writing. Do not get stuck on any one kind of punctuation. Use all of them.

Remember. First, we talked about the period and then the comma; next came the semicolon and even more than that: the colon appeared along with out-of-sight hyphens—remember the dash—and "zillions" of quotation marks and *all kinds* of italics (don't forget the parentheses and apostrophes). Understand? Great!

I have listed below a few sentences which I invite you to punctuate. Take these with you to impress your friends at parties. Or just carry them always for those moments when you need an emotional lift. Don't spend too much time on any one sentence however. 128 variations may overwhelm your friends. For a start, you might try for two.

Try to control your enthusiasm as you consider the following:

Give the bird to my cousin Ralph

That that is is that that is not is not

There are three kinds of lies lies damned lies and statistics

I can can can but I cant cant can you

He said hold it softly

Poles poles are the greatest

A woman without her man is lost

I can't resist doing that last sentence. What you have is:

A woman without her man is lost.

or

A woman: without her, man is lost.

For my money, excitement like that comes second only to long division or organ music at roller skating rinks.

The lesson from all this is that punctuation is not a series of dumb rules designed to control your prose. *YOU* use and control punctuation to clarify what you want to say. Don't be afraid of it.

FOR EXAMPLE

I'm going to take a common sentence and punctuate it several different ways, explaining how the meanings change in each case. You'll be amazed. Consider the simple statement:

You have poison ivy so don't do anything rash.

There are a few options at no cost in meaning, such as a comma between "ivy" and "so," which would give the reader a chance to pause. If I'm in the mood for a semicolon, I would delete "so" and write:

You have poison ivy; don't do anything rash.

Now, if I want to put extra emphasis on the fact that you should not do anything rash, I would write:

You have poison ivy—don't do anything rash.
or
You have poison ivy: don't do anything rash.

If I have just found out that you have poison ivy, I would write:

You have poison ivy? Don't do anything rash.

If I want to make sure that you get the joke by pointing out the play on words, I would write:

You have poison ivy, so don't do anything "rash."

If I'm embarrassed at how corny the joke is, I would write:

You have poison ivy (so don't do anything rash).

If I write:

You have poison, Ivy, so don't do anything rash.

it means that I know a lady named Ivy who is considering doing something awful to herself.

HOW A MANUSCRIPT FINDS
A PUBLISHER

June 10, 1975

Dear Mr. Myatt:

This is amusing and effective. Generally I think your advice is sound and your form appealing. But since it is addressed to students, CE is not the ideal place for it. In order to use it, teachers would have to Xerox or ditto it at some expense and nuisance, and would have the usual dilemma about getting permission or winging it.

I think that it would make a good pamphlet on XXXX's publications list. If you agree that it would be more readily available that way, write to Xxxx Xxxxx, XXXX, submit the manuscript to him, and feel free to say I suggested it. If you prefer, I'll write him, but there really isn't any advantage in that, since the decision is made by the publications board in any case.

Thanks for sending this to us, and good luck in getting it published by XXXX or by another means.

Sincerely,

Richard Ohmann, Editor
College English

June 16, 1975

Dear Mr. Myatt:

Re: "One Approach to Punctuation"

I respect Dick Ohmann's judgement at least as much as you do, but in his reply to you he evidently forgot an established policy of XXXX publications: we may not publish instructional materials for students below the pre-professional level. So, whether it would be a useful XXXX pamphlet is not an admissible issue, since we may not publish it, regardless of merit.

As an ex-English teacher, I agree with Dick that your approach is fresh. The direct exposition and the exercise work characterize the kind of material that is typically published by commercial educational publishers. In this sense, you may wish to get the reaction of the few Bay Area elhi publishing houses; I can think offhand of Xxxxxxx and Xxxxxxx-Xxxxxx; probably you can find more in *LMP*.

Thank you for thinking of XXXX as your publisher. Your manuscript is enclosed.

Cordially,

Director of Publications

July 1, 1975

Dear Mr. Myatt:

Xx Xxxxxx referred your manuscript, entitled "One Approach to Punctuation," to me. (An example of the excessive use of commas.)

I read it with pleasure, as others have; and came to the same conclusion they did. (Use of that semi-colon increases my lifetime average for semi-colons batted in to .500. No record when compared to James and Conrad, but better than the combined lifetime averages of Ruth and Aaron, I'd bet.) Xxxxxxx-Xxxxxx has no appropriate market for your materials. As you may know, we tend to provide major programs to schools. Short, inexpensive pieces such as yours would be overshadowed by the kinds of materials we publish.

This is not to comment on the merit of the fresh approach you have taken. It is only to say that our marketing and sales efforts are directed toward another kind of material.

Perhaps you will have patience enough to send your ms to Xxxxxx. They publish teacher and student materials for this kind of market.

Thank you for thinking of Xxxxxxx-Xxxxxxx. (With women's lib and our English tradition, you might want to give practice in hyphenating names.) My best wishes for your success.

Sincerely,

Editor in Chief

July 7, 1975

Dear Mr. Myatt:

RE: "One Approach to Punctuation"

Xxxxxx Publishers must join the list of those who have read
your material, but cannot publish it.

From our point of view your manuscript is a personal, rather
than a publisher's approach. It is for this reason that it is
enjoyable and effective, but not marketable as part of the
Xxxxxx line directed toward either teachers of elementary
school children, or elhi students with substantial learning
problems as opposed to lack of skills.

I believe I am correct in saying that Xxxxx's will sometimes
publish work of a tried and useful nature that might not fit
into the specific lines of a more categorized publisher.

Thank you for writing to Xxxxxx Publishers.

Sincerely,

Managing Editor

August 6, 1975

Dear Bill:

   Thank you for having me consider your item for publication. However, having read through this material found it
interesting. However, it is not enough material to make it
profitable in the market. It would be a good introduction to
a book of reproducable worksheets using each of these
examples as in introduction to each punctuation assignment. If
you would consider putting this into a group of about 48
pages I would be happy to talk to you about it.

   I will be back from vacation after August 15th and you can
contact me.

                    Yours truly

                    Publisher

August 9, 1975

Dear William,

We like your manuscript, "Punctuation" and we would like to publish it in book form. We think that the work will be a valuable and effective aid to students and teachers everywhere. Your approach is fun.

It will be a challenge to see if we can get the finished book in the hand of students where it belongs. We will certainly try hard and you will have to work with us to find sympathetic outlets.

We can publish limited subject books (that we feel are important) which other publishers will not touch, because we are a small independent press. There is a good market for these small books and we know from our experience with our other titles that people like them and need them.

Warmly,

Christine Thresh
Publisher

ABOUT THE AUTHOR

Bill Myatt, presently a part-time English teacher and a full-time truck driver, formerly a field laborer, irrigator, railroad telegrapher, real estate clerk, warehouseman, piano teacher, inventor and drug store department manager, was born in 1948 in Denver, Colorado. He attended the University of Southern California and earned his B.A. in English at the University of California, Los Angeles. While in school he married his best friend, Susan. They now live in Sonoma County with their two children, Michael and Amy. He earned his M.A. in English from California State College, Sonoma. Bill has written some bad poetry, a reasonably good play and is currently working on a screenplay. This is his first book.

His fascination with punctuation began with his stage debut in a 4th grade school play. His speaking part, "Someone's at the door! It must be Pa!" led to his discovery (while waiting in the wings) that these dramatic lines could be punctuated 128 different ways.